Heartbeat of Hope
One Family's Journey through a
High Risk Pregnancy

by Amanda Ogle

ISBN 978-0-578-02989-4

Library of Congress Control Number: 2009906172

The sweetest sound you'll ever hear is your blood beating in another's heart.

Table of Contents

Heartbeat of Hope
One Family's Journey through a
High Risk Pregnancy

Acknowledgement

This book would not be possible without our beautiful children Jake and Maddie. They provide endless stories that will melt your heart, bring you to tears, and make you laugh until your sides hurt. Kids, Mommy apologizes in advance for any embarrassing childhood moments I write about. Someday I hope that your babies will give you as much material to work with as you have given me. Our family would not be complete if it weren't for Brandon. He came into my life ready to love Jake as his own, and I have the utmost admiration for him. Brandon, you are the love of my life, and I thank you from the bottom of my heart for giving me the most precious little girl. It was a long road, and I wouldn't have survived it without you. As you always have been; you are my lighthouse. I love you.

4

Chapter 1

And Baby Makes 4

It was May 9, 2008, the day that started a long emotional roller coaster, the day I found out I was pregnant! Brandon had recently moved back to Las Vegas from Orlando and moved in with me. I had a three year old little boy named Jacob from my first marriage and had suffered two miscarriages already, the most recent just a month before this baby was conceived. The heartbreak from those miscarriages haunted me throughout this pregnancy and still remains to this day.

Several weeks before we found out we were pregnant, I had been feeling a little funny. Jake had been in the hospital with MRSA so I was preoccupied with taking care of him, but once Jake was discharged I was able to pay more attention to how I was feeling. I didn't have the classic morning sickness like I did with Jake but that mother's intuition told me that I should take a pregnancy test. Not only did I take one test, but I took eight! The first few came back negative but I knew in my heart that we had been given another chance. Test number seven had a faint positive result, so I rushed to take Jake to school and ran to the nearest drugstore for a digital test that would undoubtedly tell me YES or NO. The possibility of having another child made me happy. I've always wanted a large family, and I loved the idea of having a baby with Brandon. We had discussed trying for a baby when Jake turned five or six, but this was a little sooner than planned.

There I sat in the drugstore restroom with the test in hand, anxiously watching the blinking hourglass as what seemed like an eternity passed. PREGNANT! I believe I let out a small scream and probably startled a few people but I didn't care. We were having a baby!!! I hurried through the store to find tissue paper, a baby bottle and a bib that said "I love my Daddy!" and rushed to work. Now usually there is the notion of having a romantic dinner, and telling your husband that he's going to be a father over candle light but I just couldn't contain myself. Brandon's birthday was in two weeks and we were going to Hawaii. I contemplated waiting to tell him there, but didn't want to put a wild spin on the week, so I called him at his office and asked if he could meet me for lunch. I placed the bib inside the baby bottle and wrapped it up. I even wrapped up the pregnancy test just as reinforcement.

I was incredibly nervous, Brandon had said before that he didn't want children but then he changed his mind. I wondered if faced with the reality of being a father what his reaction would be. Would he panic? Would he be upset? I could see how much he loved Jake so I hoped that having a child of his own would excite him.

Lunch time came and I met him at a fast food joint. In the parking lot, I nervously handed him a poem about all kinds of wonderful traits, each that belonged to a father. It felt like it took an eternity for him to read it as I watched the color leave his face and his 6'4" frame waver in front of me. He took the wrapped bottle from my hand and opened it, took one look at the baby bottle and with a tone of utter disbelief he replied, "Really." He tossed the bottle into the seat of his car. I was crushed. I knew this hadn't come at the most opportune time, we had both recently been divorced and he was re-establishing himself here in Vegas after a year in Orlando, FL; but he could at least pretend to be happy.

I handed him the wrapped pregnancy test. He said, "What's this, the proof?" I wanted to punch him in the stomach and leave. I had written "Baby Ogle" on the pregnancy test with permanent marker and when he saw that he seemed to soften a little bit. We walked inside and ordered our lunch. I sat at the table on the verge of tears silently watching the man that I loved coming to terms with biology… and then it happened. The corners of his mouth started to turn up and he smiled! We began to talk about what we needed to do to prepare and talked about whether we wanted a boy or a girl, and we both agreed that having a girl frightened us.

I felt my first wave of nausea and didn't know if it was from the pregnancy itself or the act of telling Brandon we were having a baby. We weren't married, so of course that was the first thing Brandon said we needed to do. I would have loved to marry him right then and there but I didn't want to do it just because we were having a baby. We were committed to each other and we were a family, with or without a marriage license.

As we each pulled away from the restaurant headed back to our offices, I received a text from Brandon. "I'm gonna be a Daddy!" At that moment I knew that everything would be alright, at least for a while. We each went back to work and I felt like I was on cloud nine. I was having Brandon's baby and I couldn't be more excited! I could only imagine what was going through Brandon's mind at the same time.

We got home from work that night and I gave Brandon a hard time about his reaction to the news. He told me that he was having a really hectic day at work and being invited to lunch was a welcome break from the stress at the office; he wasn't in the mind set to receive the biggest news of his life! I felt badly for telling him the way that I had, but I couldn't take it back. For weeks after that I teased him for acting aloof when he found out he was going to be a father. Do I wish he had reacted differently? Sure I do, but that was one moment in our entire pregnancy…he quickly accepted the reality that our lives were going to change forever, and he actually seemed excited about it once the initial shock wore off.

He was very attentive and interested in what was happening with me and his future child right from the start. I had an old book from my pregnancy with Jake and every time I turned around Brandon was reading it. In fact, there were times when I wanted to refresh my memory about something and I had to wait until he was finished with the book before I could do my research! I wasn't about to take it away from him, after all; this was his first experience as a father. I wanted him to absorb as much of it as he wanted to.

At one point while he was doing some reading on fatherhood and his role throughout the pregnancy; he came across a chapter that told fathers that a hammock would make their spouse more comfortable during the pregnancy. He was very excited about the possibility that he could offer me some comfort and came bouncing into the bedroom to tell me the news. He wanted to remove one of the couches in the living room and install a hammock for me to rest in. You can imagine the look of shock on my face when he concluded his vision for rearranging the living room. I laughed and told him I didn't care how uncomfortable I was, there would never be a hammock in my living room. Of course after I said that I felt bad because he was genuinely interested in my comfort and didn't care how off the wall an idea sounded. Needless to say we did not install any new fixtures to the living room to aid in my comfort.

Chapter 2

Pregnant in Paradise

12

For Brandon's 30th birthday we planned a trip to Hawaii to enjoy a little bit of paradise. About 6 weeks prior to the trip we learned that our airline had filed for bankruptcy. I was so stressed out! I didn't want anything to ruin his birthday, so I frantically tried to get a refund from my credit card company in order to book new tickets. What an ordeal! Everyone was trying to book new flights, and prices were going up by the minute. After a day of negotiating with travel agencies and credit card companies we finally booked new arrangements.

The day of our departure arrived and while the plane trip was long, and although I was only a few weeks pregnant it was uncomfortable. I've never liked using airplane restrooms so I held it until we landed! Thankfully I didn't have much morning sickness; otherwise I would have made my fellow passengers very unhappy on that long flight. We got to Hawaii late in the evening, checked into our hotel and made our way through the beautiful property. Although it was dark the tiki torches throughout the resort created the most breathtaking atmosphere and the humidity in the air was such a change from what we were accustomed to. We located our room and opened the door to the balcony. Our room had an amazing view of a lagoon and a good portion of the beach. I could tell that this vacation was going to be one to remember forever. We made plans for activities the next day and turned in for bed.

We had wanted to go parasailing and hike Diamondhead but being pregnant means you take extra precautions – especially after two miscarriages. The beautiful beaches on the other hand were calling my name. I've only lived in land locked states, so being on a beach has always been a welcome change for me. Brandon on the other hand used to spend his free time in Florida at the beach whenever possible. I envied him for that! It was Brandon's birthday so I wanted him to get to do anything he wanted. As I lay on the beach working on a soon-to-be nasty sunburn he went for a swim. I love everything about the ocean except swimming in it. Being in the ocean makes me panic, but Brandon looked like he was having so much fun that I went in anyway. He swam out a bit from shore and I waded out about waist deep next to a jetty. I loved the way the salt water felt on my skin, and there is nothing more relaxing to me than the smell of the ocean; but all I could think about was what was swimming around under the surface of the water.

We went back to our towels on the sand and soaked up a bit of sun. I rolled over and noticed a collection of tiny seashells peeking out of the sand next to my beach towel. I mentioned them to Brandon and we both started digging through the sand to see who could find the smallest shells. It sounds silly that this is what we were doing on our vacation, but isn't that the point of a vacation? Finding something so utterly mindless to do was extremely refreshing.

We gathered up our things and wandered down the length of Waikiki Beach. At one point the sidewalk ends and you have to walk through the sand if you want to continue. Pregnancy can cause you to lose your breath occasionally and walking through beach sand for long stretches sure doesn't help! We took our time and walked the length of the beach then walked back. We went back to our room and washed the sand and salt off and grabbed a light lunch.

I had scheduled a massage for Brandon as part of his birthday celebration. We went to the spa on property and he got checked in. While he was enjoying his pampering session I got to go shopping! I wanted to get something unique for Jake. Ukuleles may not be unique in Hawaii, but they sure are in Nevada! I found a small inexpensive souvenir ukulele and purchased one for my boy. Brandon has a guitar and Jake was very intrigued with it, so I figured he would be excited to have something to play as well. I made my way back to the spa and read the newspaper in the lobby while I waited for Brandon to finish his massage session. When he emerged from the room he looked so relaxed. We made our way back to our room and started getting ready for our dinner reservations.

That night we went to a very popular beachfront restaurant named Duke's. We were seated outside overlooking the beach and while we were waiting for our meal to arrive we were surprised to see a fireworks display out in the ocean. From my understanding when I booked our reservations, the fireworks were usually scheduled for the weekend, but this was mid week. Brandon looked over at me and smiled and I joked that I had set up the fireworks show as well.   This was the perfect evening for a romantic birthday celebration. When we got back to the room a birthday cake and a tray of chocolate dipped fruit and truffles were waiting for us. There was also a small bottle of cognac, and although Brandon made a promise not to drink, I insisted that he have a toast. What a nice way to celebrate his 30th birthday! This was the first trip to Hawaii for both of us, and I can't think of a better reason to go!

The next day we rented a car and drove around the entire island. The island seemed beautifully endless as we drove and drove. It started to rain halfway through the drive and of course I immediately had to pee. We pulled into the Polynesian Cultural Center and paid $5.00 to park. The rain was beginning to come down harder, and we didn't have umbrellas. We didn't have tickets to see any of the exhibits, so I hurried to use the restroom and we left. That was the most expensive restroom break I've ever had! My favorite part of the drive was when we visited the North Shore; it was so peaceful and beautiful. The shoreline looked so different than Waikiki Beach. It was rocky and the sand was a completely different texture and color than what we had seen thus far in the trip. It was nice to get to enjoy parts of the island that didn't have vacation resorts right on the beach. We stopped at a little restaurant and had some appetizers, best teriyaki chicken I've ever had!! We also went to the Dole Pineapple plant and took what turned out to be my favorite picture of us. I had never seen a pineapple plant before, and I certainly didn't realize there were so many types of pineapples. During this week I couldn't get enough of the fresh pineapple and pineapple juice, I ordered it with every meal. It's a wonder I still had taste buds at the end of the week!

We stopped to look at sea turtles and checked out a bay that we would return to for snorkeling later that week. Ah, snorkeling, can't forget to mention the most comical part of our vacation. Imagine a pregnant woman who is afraid of the ocean – and claustrophobic! Now picture her snorkeling for the first time. Priceless! I panicked and cut my hand on coral reef, I couldn't get back to the beach fast enough. Brandon stayed in the water while I nursed my wounded ego from the shore. While I was setting up my blanket and cooler, I heard another girl scream from out in the reef. She had unexpectedly startled an eel and it scared her to pieces and she made the same quick return to the shore that I did. Can't say that I blame her, I probably would have grown wings to get out of the water if I had seen an eel. We spent about seven hours at the bay and I ended up getting one heck of a sun burn. We were exhausted by the time we were picked up by the shuttle. Surprisingly I didn't have to use the restroom as much as I expected that day, and it's a good thing because it was quite a hike to get to one!

The island of Oahu is beautiful especially once you get outside the city. We visited Pearl Harbor and paid our respects. We were both overcome by emotion and deeply touched by the sheer number of visitors who stood in line with us. I was able to control my tears until a young girl, probably eight years old, opened a lei and dropped orchids one by one over the USS Arizona. That simple gesture caught the attention of several adults around her and we were touched by her thoughtfulness. The scent of the oil from the Arizona permeated the air and burned into our nostrils. It was amazing that after all of these years you can still smell that oil, what a haunting reminder of what lay beneath the surface of the water. We walked through the museum and looked at all of the artifacts from those who had died. They were all so young, and had mothers just like me. I thought of my own children, said a prayer for those who were lost and we headed back to our hotel.

We walked around the resort picking out souvenirs for our family and friends. I had been eyeing the pearl kiosk every time we walked past it and really wanted to pick out a pearl for the baby. We didn't know if we were having a boy or a girl yet, but I figured a pearl truly signified the tiny baby that was growing inside me either way. We picked an oyster and went through the ritual to open it. The lady at the kiosk cleaned it and told us that the color of the pearl symbolized prosperity. What a great fortune for our baby! We picked up a few more items and tucked them away in our carry on luggage so that we wouldn't lose them during our flight back home.

Our week in Hawaii was relaxing and a wonderful opportunity for us to enjoy being alone together. I am thankful that I wasn't much farther along in the pregnancy than I was, and happy that I wasn't dealing with much morning sickness at that point. We were able to enjoy the vacation with only a few modifications. We agreed that next time we visit the islands we would stay on Maui. With two children I don't know when that trip will happen but I look forward to it nonetheless!

18

Chapter 3

Heartbeat of Hope

When we got back home we planned on telling our parents about the baby and shortly after that we went to our first prenatal visit with the OBGYN. Now I know what you're thinking, why on earth would we tell people when we've just endured the pain of miscarriage? You're right but the excitement was too much to bear. Our first visit with the doctor was a normal check up, all of the initial questions, exam etc. Our due date was January 18, 2009.

Now it was time to figure out how to tell our families. I had found a cartoon image of a positive pregnancy test and e-mailed it to my sister. She opened the e-mail at my parent's house and called them over to look. My parents were shocked but excited too. They wanted a granddaughter since they had three grandsons already. It's funny because my parents only had my sister and me. No boys. When Jake was born they were so excited because they got to enjoy having a little boy around. Then my nephews were born and they got to enjoy even MORE little boys running around. Now they wanted a little girl. I wondered if they had forgotten the trouble my sister and I caused for them as we were growing up. I sure hadn't forgotten about it! To be honest, I had flashbacks of all the things I tried to get away with as a kid and it horrified me that I could have a daughter that would do the same kinds of things…if not worse!

I hadn't met Brandon's family yet, and we were going back to Missouri so that I could meet them. Boy was I nervous. Meeting his family for the first time AND telling them we were having a baby, the pressure was on! We made a small photo album for his Mom with pictures of Jake, Las Vegas, the animals, and the hospital that Jake was born in. Then we added a copy of the first ultrasound picture of our baby and put it on a pink piece of paper. We added the words "Sugar and Spice and Everything Nice". We didn't know what the baby's sex was but Brandon's mom had mentioned that she wished she had a granddaughter. I hoped we weren't going out on a limb, but it was worth it.

We arrived in Missouri and headed to Brandon's Mom's house. I was so nervous. She walked out and greeted us and we all went back inside the house. I could tell Brandon was nervous to by the way he was acting and talking to his Mom. He handed her the photo album and told her that we had put together some pictures to share with her. We wanted to show her what our life was like back in Las Vegas. She flipped through the pages and when she got to the final page she stopped. Her jaw dropped and she said, "Is this a joke?" We told her it wasn't a joke, we were having a baby. She asked if it was a girl, and we told her we didn't know yet. She started to cry and Brandon held out his arms to hug her. She walked right past him and came to hug me. I was shocked! Brandon's face was priceless; he looked happy and left out all at the same time. It was funny! When his stepdad Jimmy got home, his Mom showed him the photo album and told him that they were going to be grandparents again.

We stayed at their house until after midnight that night and we were exhausted, but it was worth it. We talked about Brandon's childhood and looked through pictures of him as a baby. I was so relieved that they accepted me and the fact that we were having a baby so early in our relationship, it took a lot of weight off our shoulders.

The next day we went to see Brandon's Dad and his stepmom Katy. His Dad collects coins and also sells items on eBay, so we had a coin made for him with engraving on each side. We took a picture of the coin and posted it on eBay just like a normal listing. When we arrived at their house, we had Katy look up an item that we came across and thought was cool. They both looked at the screen and tried to figure out what it was, and Brandon pulled the real coin out of his pocket and handed to them. They were so excited!

Nobody expected Brandon to have children, so I think they were a bit amazed that he was so happy about the baby and prepared to be a father. I know I was impressed with him! Both his Dad and his Mom were happy to find out that they were having another grandchild, and were so kind to me. I was so relieved that they accepted the situation and me with open arms.

We told his brother and his sister that there was going to be another baby in the family and they were excited too. Brandon's brother has a boy and a girl, and his sister has two little girls of her own. I felt like I was home visiting my own family on that trip, it was so pleasant and relaxing. We visited with Brandon's Grandma as well and told her the news. She makes quilts and she told us to let her know if we were having a boy or a girl, she was going to have a quilt ready for us.

She took us into a back bedroom and showed me the quilts that she had made, including a photo album of the quilts she had completed and had given away. I was reminded of my own Grandmother, as I had spent my entire childhood watching her piece together beautiful quilts by hand. I felt like she was right there with me as I pointed out the quilt that she had made for me when I was little; Grandma's flower garden. Then I saw the log cabin design and the wedding ring quilt.

It took all that I had not to start crying, I was so moved. I was happy that my baby would get to enjoy the beauty of a quilt that was made with love. I wished that my Grandma was still alive so that she could share in the joy of this new life. Jake had been conceived shortly after she passed away and she didn't get the opportunity to meet the child that I had wanted for years. Now I was having another baby and those feelings of sadness came back as I pictured how happy she would be to have another great-grandchild.

I was so glad that we visited with Brandon's Grandma, sharing that time with her was one of my favorite moments on our trip back to Missouri. As we left her house she gave me a hug and Brandon told me that seeing her do that made him feel so good. He was happy that his family liked me so much, and wanted to bring Jake back someday so that they could meet him too!

Now we were getting excited about whether we were having a boy or a girl. We wondered if Jake would have a brother or sister to grow up with and were curious how he would handle either of them. Somewhere we had read that if a pregnant woman eats lots of bananas and has breakfast in the mornings she might be able to influence the sex of a baby and have a little boy. We are both intelligent people and know how the baby's sex is determined but we thought it was worth a try. I ate so many bananas I quickly grew sick of them. Finally I threw in the hat and decided that the baby would be whatever he or she was meant to be. Just thinking about bananas now makes my stomach turn.

We came to terms with the fact that if we had a little girl it wouldn't be the end of the world and might be fun! I

24

chided Brandon that I wanted at least three more children, so if this baby was a girl we would still have other chances to have a boy. He just laughed and told me that we needed to get through this pregnancy first before we started talking about having more. He was right, but I always tend to have the big picture in mind instead of dealing with the here and now.

Our second visit with our OBGYN was not as pleasant as the first. I climbed up on the table and prepared for the cool jelly for the Doppler so that we could listen to the baby's heartbeat. The doctor couldn't find anything using the Doppler and as we sat with our hearts in our throats she left the room to get an ultrasound machine. As she wheeled it next to the exam table I fought the urge to cry, this couldn't be happening again. All of the pain from the miscarriages came flooding back through my mind as she searched with ultrasound for the baby's heartbeat.

She still couldn't find a heartbeat and the monitor was pushed away from us. We couldn't even see our baby. Even though she knew we had experienced miscarriages the doctor didn't do much to make us feel better. She said sometimes that happens and sent us on our way. We had no idea if everything looked ok, or if there was a problem with our baby. I was furious with her and scared that we were possibly going to face losing this child. Needless to say, I immediately started looking for a new OBGYN and it proved a wise choice.

That afternoon, we called a local 3D ultrasound clinic to get some peace of mind and they were kind enough to take us as a walk in. We explained my history and the owner of the clinic said not to worry, but reminded me that she couldn't give any medical diagnosis or advice. That was fine with us; we just wanted to SEE our baby. She quickly found the baby and focused on the heartbeat. I was 14 weeks pregnant. She let us listen to the heartbeat for nearly 20 minutes as we both cried. The baby looked like a tiny alien but was beautiful to us. Then, she asked if we wanted to know the sex, adding that at this point in the pregnancy she couldn't guarantee anything. Of course we did, we were so elated that everything looked ok! Amazingly the answer appeared as plain as day, we were having a baby girl! Words can not express the gratitude that we felt for the kindness we received at that ultrasound clinic, and we are forever grateful. We continued to visit the clinic throughout our pregnancy.

On the drive home we called our parents and told them that they were having a granddaughter. This baby is the first granddaughter on my side and the first granddaughter for Brandon's mom so it was very big news. I was quite proud that I was able to have the first girl, even though the thought of a pre-teen daughter was racing through my mind a million miles a second. I knew the kind of hell I put my folks through; I just imagined that she would give me a run for my money! At the same time I was glad that our daughter would have a big brother, I had always wished I had an older brother myself. I had no idea what to do to prepare for a baby girl, but there was time to figure it out.

I worried that Brandon was a little let down that he wasn't having a boy of his own. He explained that he got along so well with girls; he knew he could handle having a daughter. He relived how much he enjoyed taking care of his sister when she was a baby, and how his favorite thing to do was brushing her hair. That made me feel better, he was handling the news a lot better than I was. I knew what to expect with little boys. They are rough and they like dirt. They do gross things and make you laugh at them. They remind you of little old men, and sometimes they remind you of little old cranky men. What was I supposed to expect with a daughter? I know how moody and irritated I get and the thought of having two of us in the house acting like crazy women really scared me.

I remember how much my mom, sister and I struggled to get along in our house growing up and I felt sorry for my Dad for having to survive that as the only male. Even the animals were female! At least Brandon would have Jake and the dog to even things out with the male to female ratio at our house. I started thinking about all things pink; I hated the color pink and swore that no daughter of mine would wear that wretched color. (Pink was my sister's favorite color growing up, and I think that's where my disgust for the shade came from.) My favorite color as a child was purple, it didn't matter what shade it was but if something belonged to me it had to be purple! We decided that the baby's color scheme would be lavender and light yellow and we would decorate with dragonflies. Hopefully she won't hate us for the choices we made. Knowing my luck her favorite color will be pink!

Chapter 4

What's in a Name?

28

Now that we knew what the baby's sex was, it was time to pick names. How hard is it to pick a name for a child? For us it was excruciating. There is so much pressure to pick a name your child won't hate you for later in life, but is unique enough that every kid on the block won't share the same name. Brandon and I had a name picked out right away if we were having a boy. Logan Jesse Ogle. Of course we couldn't decide on a girl's name and that's what we were having. We agreed that her middle name would be Elizabeth after my best friend, but we didn't know what first name would suit her. More importantly, we didn't know what first name would suit her Daddy.

I had names that I liked and any one of them would have been fine with me but each time I would mention one to Brandon he would wrinkle his nose and repeat it with a tone of disgust. He was driving me crazy. I would get angry with him and told him that we couldn't have a child with no name; we needed to pick something already. Back and forth we went, and looking back I don't think he made any suggestions himself, he just kept shooting mine down.

Sometimes at work a name would catch my eye and I would e-mail him to see if he liked it; each time it would be met with disapproval from my better half. Finally I started sending off the wall names of trees and objects just to frustrate him enough to get his attention. My plan backfired and he just laughed at me, that's usually what happens when I try to strong arm him. And then it hit me; Madelyn. It was classy, elegant, feminine and not the name of a tree. He had to love it! I e-mailed him and he responded immediately. He loved it! Our daughter would be Madelyn Elizabeth Ogle, Maddie for short. We told Jake and he began calling my belly *Baby Madwin.*

Now we could move on with the pregnancy – she had a name! This little person inside me was beginning to have an identity of her own. Slowly I was coming to terms that I was having a little girl and I was enjoying the fact that this pregnancy was going smoothly. I felt good, had hardly any morning sickness and looked forward to experiencing all of the "firsts" throughout this pregnancy with Brandon. I was really excited and re-read all of my pregnancy books to refresh my memory. I even bought a few new books, a lot had changed in the five years since I was pregnant with Jake; or at least it felt like a lot had changed!

It felt good to be pregnant again. This time I felt like I knew what I was doing and was ahead of the game. With Jake, everything was brand new so all of the changes that my body went through were a bit unnerving. Experiencing things for the first time is exciting and scary at the same time. Now I felt confident in my ability to carry a baby as well as my ability to be a mother. This was going to be a piece of cake!

Chapter 5

The Diagnosis

Right as I reached 18 weeks I was scheduled to see our new OBGYN. The weekend before my appointment I noticed that my face felt flushed and it looked as though my cheeks had been slapped. I thought nothing of it as I'm a red head with fair skin; sometimes I look a bit flushed. The next morning I learned that the remainder of our pregnancy was going to be an uphill battle. I woke up with painful joints and a lacy rash covering my body. I had my suspicions and looked through my pregnancy books to find the list of diseases and symptoms to watch out for. I suspected I had fifth disease. Fifth disease is a childhood disease similar to measles, mumps, rubella, and chicken pox. It is the "fifth" disease that children sometimes contract. I've seen fifth disease before, and several days earlier I had seen the same type of rash on my son but attributed it to his eczema. Every symptom that I read about regarding fifth disease fit the symptoms that I was experiencing. If I was right, I had been exposed to a virus that is potentially fatal to fetuses, especially if contracted by the mother prior to 20 weeks gestation. I called my new OBGYN that Monday morning and informed them of my symptoms so that they could test me right away at my appointment. Sure enough, I tested positive. I was numb.

Four weeks had passed since we struggled to hear our daughter's heartbeat and we had spent the next four weeks elated that we were out of the woods, now this. I was at a point where women begin to show and start to get that glow of pregnancy, but I was grief stricken that there was a chance this baby may not make it. We were referred to a perinatologist and began appointments with her every two weeks in addition to our normal visits with the OBGYN. Brandon was my rock, he went to every appointment and held me at night when all I could do was cry. I researched the virus, the statistics, and bravely searched for images of the affect it could have on a fetus. I had to know everything there was to know. Those images are forever burned in my mind and I wish that I hadn't found them because for the next 19 weeks they haunted me in my dreams.

Our first visit with the perinatologist was something we weren't prepared for. I think in some ways we tried to pretend that everything was ok, this was just a technicality but deep down in our core we both knew the seriousness of each appointment. We arrived early for the appointment and were told that we had to meet with a genetic counselor prior to meeting with the doctor. We went across the street from the medical center and tried to grab a bite to eat even though we were a bit stunned by the idea of meeting with a genetic counselor. Although the risk to the baby was caused by my exposure to a virus and not genetic, every possible family illness was racing through my head. Suddenly all of the questions regarding birth defects and developmental problems were in the forefront of my mind. My head was spinning; I didn't know what to think.

For two hours we met with the genetic counselor and she covered everything from Down's syndrome to our cancer risk. I was 28, Brandon had just turned 30 and we were both otherwise healthy individuals. After taking an extremely extensive family history from us she found that our statistics were in favor of us having a healthy baby if we could just get past the exposure to fifth disease. We were told that exposure to fifth disease at this point in pregnancy can cause an infection resulting in fetal loss. Our risk for losing the baby was around 10%. Had I been exposed after 20 weeks gestation, that risk drops to around 1%. Ten percent doesn't sound like a huge risk, but when you've already had miscarriages you look forward to making it past 12 weeks for the hope of reducing your chances of losing the baby. I was in the clear as far as that went, but now I had a whole new obstacle to overcome.

Next we met with our perinatologist. Our time with her lasted for nearly an hour and a half and she explained that although it is rare that a baby is harmed by fifth disease, they take every precaution and adjust the frequency of appointments as needed. Fifth disease can cause inflammation in the baby's heart and damage bone marrow causing a lack of red blood cells. This causes anemia, and if the infection is severe hydrops can occur, which is excessive fluid in the baby's bodily tissues that can result in fetal death. Based upon results of each office visit, the doctor would determine if we needed to come back in one week or if we could wait two weeks to be seen again. Ok, I thought, in a few weeks they will find out that we are in the clear and we can go back to our normally scheduled prenatal visits. Boy was I wrong.

At first we saw the doctor every two weeks, and during those visits she would do a routine ultrasound that measured the growth of our little girl from her head to her little toes and monitored her for fluid build up around her heart as well as in her face and extremities, a sign of fetal hydrops. This part of the visit was our sanctuary. We got to see her, hear her and imagine who she was going to look like. We were always given new ultrasound pictures, and considering the amount of times we went to appointments, we could probably have wallpapered her nursery with them! After the routine ultrasound the mood would shift. This is when the technician would locate the baby's head and use the ultrasound to measure the blood flow in the vessels of her brain. The baby would

never stay still for this part and it became her "little game".
We anxiously watched the monitor trying to decipher the
spikes in her blood flow before we were told what the
measurements meant. We didn't really know what we were
looking at, but we were trying to absorb as much as we could
during our visits.

When a fetus is exposed to fifth disease there are two
ways the doctor can monitor for anemia. They can either do a
blood draw from the baby's umbilical cord by amniocentesis
and test it, or they can monitor the blood flow via ultrasound.
If a baby is anemic the blood flow is measured at a faster rate
than it should be. Our perinatologist chose to do ultrasounds
and told us we were lucky that technology was so advanced;
just a few years ago she would have done an amnio every week
to check the baby. We were also told that if the baby was
anemic I may have to undergo an intrauterine blood
transfusion, and if I was far enough along for the baby to be
delivered she would have a blood transfusion after birth. The
thought of that scared us to death.

In the first few visits the tests showed an elevated
blood flow and the doctor had us come back two weeks later.
At 24 weeks the tests showed an unexpected spike and the
doctor told us she wanted to see us weekly going forward.
That was a moment that changed my life as a mother; I felt
helpless and scared. All we could do was wait and pray for the
best. There was nothing I could do to make things better and
that is the most horrible feeling ever. I felt so bad that
Brandon's first experience as an expecting father was so
complicated and frightening and I wanted nothing more than to
go back and somehow change the fact that I had been exposed
to the virus. We wanted this to be a happy, beautiful

pregnancy and it was filled with so much worry. It took everything that I had, but I tried my hardest to pretend that I wasn't scared to death. I know Brandon wasn't fooled by my feigned courage, but it wouldn't have changed things if I had been crying all the time. There were moments when I would break down but those usually happened on the way to or from work when I was all alone. We repeated this cycle every week and cautiously climbed into the emotional roller coaster before every visit. After each appointment we would process the information that we received and try to digest what it meant. We tried to enjoy our time between appointments but it was hard to do because just as soon as we would come to terms with what the last visit showed, we had to prepare ourselves for the next one.

This was a serious test of our emotional endurance, individually and as a couple. For some couples this complication would be detrimental to the relationship, but we seemed to grow stronger because of it. We stuck together and communicated how we felt about each appointment and what our fears were regarding the weeks to come. It was nice to have someone that I could relate to, who knew exactly what I was going through. Brandon was the only person in the world that I knew could understand how I felt.

It felt like we were living every week in suspended animation. Sometimes it seemed as if we had just lived through the exact same day over and over again. 40 weeks of pregnancy can feel long enough, but when you add in complications and additional doctor's visits it makes each week crawl by. I tried not to even pay attention to what week we were in because it always felt like we should be further along than we really were. Part of that was because of the sheer number of appointments, but some of it was because I wanted to get to full term just in the hopes that Maddie would be ok. Every week that passed was one less week we had to worry about her developing complications from the virus.

Suddenly the excitement of preparing for our daughter was placed on hold. Our focus shifted from preparing for her birth to scheduling office visits. Not only did we not have the time to enjoy making plans for her arrival; it was also hard to think that far in advance when her well being was in limbo. I struggled with the idea of all the things that I should have been doing. Yes, the baby needed a crib; but I got a knot in my stomach just thinking about the possibility that we may not bring a baby home to sleep in it.

Our diagnosis and the survival of my daughter took precedence over everything else. Suddenly it no longer mattered if everything was pink. It didn't matter what name we picked for her...we just wanted her to be healthy. I've never prayed so much in my entire life. I would say a prayer every morning on my way in to work; asking that we would be granted a miracle and our daughter would be healthy. I would say the same prayer in the evening as I lay in the bath tub trying to soak away the worries of the day.

Thankfully, pregnancy makes me very tired; so although I was so stressed out that I normally wouldn't be able to sleep, the physical exhaustion was enough to knock me out on most nights. That's when the nightmares would kick in. I never had a "normal" pregnancy dream with Maddie. My dreams during this pregnancy only consisted of the horrors of fifth disease. Flashbacks of the fetal images I had seen terrorized me almost nightly. I had a hard time imagining who our daughter was going to look like because I could only picture the poor babies who hadn't survived.

Chapter 6

The Disconnected Mother

I tried to walk around all day with my hand on my belly trying desperately to feel each kick. I wanted to build a connection with my baby so badly, but at the same time was terrified that the next week might bring bad news and I would be crushed. How do you explain to other women who have had normal pregnancies that you aren't ecstatic about every doctor visit and every week that passes by? Nobody seems to understand that while this is one of life's greatest gifts we were afraid to become attached for the risk of it being taken away. Don't get me wrong I loved this baby just as much as I loved my son but I was depressed.

In many ways, I was grieving a baby that hadn't been lost and I distanced myself to avoid being hurt. I didn't want to shop for her, didn't want to decorate her nursery, and didn't want to think about any of the fun pregnancy things that mothers normally do. All I could do was bury myself in the facts. Everyone at work wanted to know why I was gone all the time for appointments. Hardly anyone had heard of fifth disease, and none knew the implications if the baby developed the virus too. That meant I had a lot of explaining to do when all I wanted to do was curl up and cry. Every morning I put on a brave face and kept going to work, it provided the distraction that I thought I needed; anything was better than wallowing in self pity and fear of the unknown.

We share custody of Jake with his father, so every other week Jake lives with us. I looked forward to those weeks because it offered a wonderful distraction. Jake is a very busy little boy. He plays hard and has millions of questions just waiting to be answered. Of course there were moments when he provided too much distraction and I was on Mommy overload; but that can happen no matter what else is going on in our lives. When Jake would go back to be with his father the house was so quiet. I always miss him when he's gone but I missed him even more during this pregnancy because he forced me to come out of my mental cave.

Each week I would get e-mail updates on the progress of our pregnancy and each time I would forward the e-mail to Brandon without reading it. Even reading developmental chapters in my baby books was excruciating; all I wanted to read about was fifth disease and what to do to get through it. I had been pregnant before and had memorized most of the milestones from my first pregnancy. I am grateful for that, because I would have truly missed out had this been my first pregnancy and I kept turning my cheek when it came to anything baby. Still I felt a bit cheated. This was my first little girl; I wasn't suffering from much morning sickness and otherwise was having a great pregnancy, I should have been ecstatic.

I wanted to be able to enjoy this with Brandon, spending nights on the couch just waiting for her to kick without a care in the world. After I had Jake, people would ask how I liked being pregnant and I would tell them that even though I had morning sickness until the day I delivered him, I would do it all over again. I loved that pregnancy and felt such guilt for wishing this pregnancy would hurry up and be over. We just wanted our little girl, enough with the pregnancy stuff already.

We had purchased one of those home heartbeat monitors so that we could listen to her little heart, but since we were always at the doctor we hardly used the one we had at home. We weren't too let down over that because getting the home monitor to work was like pulling teeth. We never even purchased a baby book for her, and we didn't receive one at our baby showers either. The thought of documenting anything at that point was a little torturous. I hoped that someday I wouldn't look back with regret that we hadn't documented anything. I'm sure some who read this will think I could have made it easier on myself if I had been more optimistic. That could be true; however it would have been easier to think positively with more time between our appointments. Having tests run every week is enough to make you a realist, let alone not allow you to absorb what happened at the last appointment. The gravity of the situation sank in each week when we would sit in the waiting room with all the other high risk mothers.

I looked at their faces, trying to read them and see if they were handling things the same way I was. I had no idea what condition they were being seen for. I felt for each of them, every woman deserves to have a wonderful happy pregnancy. Each of the women looked like this was routine for them, and maybe it was. Maybe they were stronger women than I am or maybe they were hiding their fear and concern just like I was. Some of them had their husbands with them and others were completely alone; reading magazines or watching the TV to pass the time. I felt fortunate that I always had Brandon by my side. If I had a breakdown or received news that I couldn't handle I knew that he was right there to help me through it.

Some of the women brought their entire family of children into the small waiting room. There were only about 10 chairs in this waiting room, and with four physicians in the office it filled up rather quickly. Adding an extra 3 or 4 children to the mix was sometimes a pleasant distraction and other times it was enough to make me want to pull my hair out.

I was grateful that we weren't always on the same appointment schedule as the women who always brought their young children. When I say young, I mean large strollers taking up a tiny room. I was also very irritable from the stress of the situation. The girls at the front desk liked to sit with waiting room window open and they would have the most inappropriate conversations in what every Mommy knows as an "outside voice". I can't tell you the number of times that Brandon got to see me roll my eyes, or hear me sigh so deeply I thought my lungs would collapse. Come on people, it's a doctor's waiting room, not a rock concert!

Although there was always a waiting room full of women who were high risk each week, I still felt incredibly alone. I kept telling myself that everything was going to be fine, the baby would be healthy and this would all end up being a long bad dream. I tried really hard to convince myself of that but I was struggling to believe it.

I thought about Maddie's pediatrician. I knew each of the doctor's in the pediatric group; and each of them had seen Jake at one point or another. He hadn't had many issues over the years with the exception of recurrent MRSA infections that we had finally gotten under control. I wondered how they handled babies who were born sick, and if I would feel as comfortable with their skills if Maddie was born with complications. I tried not to think about it much, I tried to have faith in their abilities yet knew that I would have no qualms about changing pediatricians if she needed better care than they could provide.

I wondered if our perinatologist would be present at the delivery, or if she would only come in if there was an emergency. I even thought about what would happen if she decided during one of our visits that I needed to have the baby immediately. As hard as it was to think about these things I was trying to be as mentally and emotionally prepared as possible under any circumstances. On the surface I looked calm and collected, but underneath my emotions were churning like a troubled sea.

Chapter 7

My Sweet Jake

Then there was my sweet Jake. Jake had wanted a baby brother or sister for a while but we weren't sure he was ready for the competition for attention. There was no turning back now, all we could do was prepare him as much as possible and plan to include him in as much as he could tolerate. With each visit to the grocery store, Jake would ask if we could get something for his baby *Madwin* before he would ask to get something for himself. This was a huge step for Jake because he always asks for something at the store. Of course we couldn't tell him no because he was being so kind and unselfish.

He would quiz us at the grocery store about the things that *Madwin* would like or dislike. Conveniently enough, in his opinion if he liked something she would like it too. We'll see if it turns out that way! He was drawn to baby toys at the store, and never really seemed to grow out of them. Sometimes that bothered us that he wasn't as interested in more age appropriate items but other times we were happy that he would be interested in playing with the baby when she arrived. We gave him a job to do…it was his job to test out her baby toys and make sure they were safe and fun enough for her to play with. He was ready for the job!

Giving Jake things to do in order for us to prepare for the baby was extremely helpful. He was so interested and ready to learn what he needed to know about babies; he made that part of our job so much easier! We even bought a small baby doll and gave to him so that he could practice being gentle. I wasn't sure how he would react to the baby doll idea but he actually loved it!

His favorite thing to do with the doll was change it's diaper. He would lay it down on the chair and crank its little legs up over its head, then he would yell, "It's got poop!" Not exactly surprising that a preschooler is enthralled with all things poop, but the thought of him doing that with a real dirty diaper made me cringe every time.

Jake learned how to give a baby a bath, and how to hold the doll so that her head wouldn't flop around. He wasn't allowed to take the doll places because we didn't have a car seat for her, and he could only hold her when he was sitting down. He even tried to give her a bottle a time or two. This practice was as good for Jake as it was for me. Seeing him pretending to take care of his soon to be sister helped me cope. Jake wasn't living in the reality that we were. He was blessed with the innocence and imagination that only a child his age could offer.

My son had no idea that there were any complications with his little sister since he was in school for almost every appointment. The few times that he went I prayed that we wouldn't receive bad news in front of him.

He is an incredibly compassionate child who is extremely protective of his Mommy, and I can't imagine what that kind of news would do to him. Keeping him from the reality as much as possible was one of the best parenting decisions I think I've made. I didn't want to spoil the experience for Jake. He told all of his friends at school about his baby, and they were all excited about it. I was torn because I wanted him to be excited, but I didn't want him to be hurt if something happened to Madelyn.

Jake was very curious about the baby. Thankfully he never asked how she got in my belly, but he sure did want to know how she would come out. Now more than ever I was glad that I had a c-section with him and would have a c-section with her. I showed him my faint c-section scar and explained that Mommy would go to the hospital and the doctor would give me a shot so I didn't hurt. Then the doctor would take a tiny knife and cut along the little white line. That's when the baby would come out. He was intrigued! Every so often he would remember that little bit of information and recite it back to me, regardless of where we were. Somewhere out there a grocery store clerk learned more about me than she wanted to! Having children will give you thick skin; I say this because shortly after our little discussion about how the baby would be born, he decided that all of his friends needed to learn too.

One morning when I dropped him off he ran right over to his pack of friends, (yes four year old boys travel in packs) and said, "Guess how the baby is gonna come out!!" He explained everything I told him and said there would be lots of blood and guts. They all yelled, "Ewwww, disgusting!" and started giggling. No wonder little girls at that age want nothing to do with boys. This "lesson" I gave Jake on childbirth came back to haunt me again when we took him to the 3D ultrasound clinic to see his baby sister.

The room was very large with a couch, some toys for siblings to play with and a large flat screen TV. I hopped up on the exam table and lifted my shirt. Jake was distracted looking for pieces to a toy, and the clinic owner squirted the warm ultrasound jelly on my stomach. She placed the Doppler on my lower abdomen and started searching for a good image. Right about then, Jake looked up to see what was going on.

His sweet blue eyes looked like they were going to pop out of his head and he turned white as a ghost. He ran over and stared at my belly. He thought his sister was going to come out right then and there, and he wasn't ready for it. I learned at that moment that little boys are all talk. It was one of the funniest moments in our pregnancy, and one that I will embarrass him with for years to come.

I also had to have a toned down version of "the talk" with him, simply to explain why only mommies grow babies in their tummies and daddies don't. He would walk around the house pushing his stomach out and rubbing it. He was convinced that he was having a baby too. We realized that diaper changes would be especially interesting since Jake is fascinated with his boy parts. We explained that his sister would have different parts than he did, and showed him his doll. She wasn't anatomically correct, but smooth doll parts look a lot more like girl babies than they do boy babies. He grasped that concept and announced it like breaking news everywhere we went. "The baby is going to have different parts, not like mine!" His declarations always drew chuckles and smiles from people around us. At least I didn't have to answer questions about the baby's sex; Jake handled that for me!

Every morning when I would take him to school a small swarm of little boys would run over and ask when I was going to take the baby out of my stomach. Their innocence and curiosity warmed my heart and sometimes those morning encounters were the only time I would smile all day. At one point, one of my son's friends told me that my belly looked like it was going to explode. I went to work and checked myself out in the restroom mirror. He was right. If he could only see the silvery stripes that remained from my first pregnancy he would have thought the baby was trying to claw her way out! Boy, if teenagers believed that theory it would be the best form of birth control known to man!

Sometimes he was oblivious to the idea that a baby would be joining our family soon, and other times that was all he could talk about. I wondered how he would react that first night at home with a crying newborn. Heck, I wondered how I would react that first night at home with a crying newborn, and I had done it before!

Jake is such a sweet child, and truly well behaved considering his age. He never has issues at school and he has the ability to charm his teachers. I was always very close to my teachers as a child, so it makes me happy to see that he behaves for them and respects them just like I used to. I hoped that Madelyn would be a lot like him. Brandon is extremely laid back, almost to the point of irritating me – so I imagined the baby having those same characteristics. I on the other hand only wish I was as laid back as he is and hoped that Madelyn didn't have my personality.

We already knew she was tough, just like her big brother. When Jake gets sick he is such a trooper. He just takes it like a man and never complains. He was amazing when he was in the hospital for MRSA. The only time he cried was when his IV migrated out of his hand and the nurse tried to reinsert it. She tried three times and on the fourth attempt I stopped her. I nearly passed out while she was going at him with the needle. Poke me all you want, but don't hurt my babies!! Jake is still traumatized from that part of his hospital stay.

He suffers from eczema, which is part of the culprit with his MRSA infections. We worried that I would end up with an infection during my pregnancy. We were very careful and each of us bathed with a special antimicrobial soap to make sure that we weren't spreading any dangerous germs. We had the carpets deep cleaned to make sure that any harmful bacteria had been eliminated, both for Jake's health and in preparation of the baby's arrival.

I thought about the baby and wondered if she was going to struggle with eczema too. My Grandpa, sister, nephews and I all have it too. Hopefully Brandon's genetic influence will prevail and we won't have to watch her go through what Jake does.

Chapter 8

Preparing for the Unexpected

As if our other complications had not been enough to handle, my history of pre-term labor reared its ugly head. I had pre-term labor with Jake, and the last time it struck with him he was born two weeks before his due date. Fortunately, Jake had no issues and I brought him home with normal concern. With Maddie, the pre-term labor struck again. This time I was placed on heart medication to relax my uterus and put on bed rest for a week.

That was one of the longest weeks of my life. I stayed on the couch mostly and tried to find a way to pre-occupy my mind. I read baby books hoping to trigger those feel good mommy feelings – only to feel like nothing was written for me. I watched shows about expecting parents and wanted to tell them to count their blessings, because they had the perfect TV pregnancies. The medication worked and I was allowed to return to work.

I continued to work even when the pre-term labor struck again at 34 weeks. I couldn't stand the thought of another week on bed rest so I convinced my doctor that I would take it easy and if things got out of hand I would let them know. Once again I was placed on medication and I tried my best to tough it out. At one point, the doctor told me I had an incompetent cervix and may need to have a stitch put in to keep me from dilating. I was relieved that we didn't need that procedure and I worked through contractions and discomfort.

I tried to avoid taking the medication at work because it messed with my heart and made me feel funny, so I attempted to stay in my office as much as possible and only get up to use the restroom and get lunch. I worked at a resort and much of the time I would have to walk to our sales floors to meet with someone but most of the time it was possible for them to come to my office or communicate by phone or e-mail. Staying seated helped the contractions, but put a lot of pressure on my sciatic nerve. I am RH negative and had to have a Rhogam shot to protect the baby. When I received that shot the nurse hit my sciatic nerve and it caused an increase in sciatic discomfort.

Every so often I would get up and walk to the break room to get a drink or use the restroom even those short walks would trigger contractions again. I knew that if I pushed it I would end up at home on the couch again and I wasn't going to let that happen. I limited my movements from my office to just getting up from my desk and going out to talk to the girls that shared the larger office with me.

At 34 weeks the perinatologist told us that she wanted to do an amnio to check the baby. We had tossed the idea around that it was always a possibility and again, I tried to be brave and say that I would have one every week if it meant that the baby would be healthy…but deep down when she said that word a chill went up my spine. It sounds crazy, but it wasn't really until then that I realized we truly were high risk. You would think that after 14 weeks of visits I would have come to terms with that fact, but when you are so deep in denial it takes a statement like that to snap you back into real life.

Brandon and I like to plan and prepare for as much as possible in life, it's a quirk that we both have, fortunately; otherwise I think it would drive us crazy. There was no time to plan when it came to the amnio. The doctor said she wanted to do one and within minutes she had a surgical tray all set up. I remember hoping that I wouldn't pass out, and being concerned that the baby would bump into the needle. She was quite the wiggler, always giving the ultrasound technician a hard time when she would try to measure her blood flow. The procedure didn't hurt much at all, and baby Maddie didn't move an inch once the needle entered my uterus. That part was a little humorous because it was like she knew it was coming.

My amniotic fluid was collected and the doctor told me that based on the appearance alone it looked like the baby hadn't started taking practice breaths yet. That was normal for this point in the pregnancy, but we were hoping she was a little advanced incase we had to take her early. As the needle left my stomach, I started to feel some pretty strong cramps but I knew that I should expect that. One bandage and a tiny puncture hole later I was good as new, at least on the outside. The amnio came back negative, and the baby's lungs weren't mature enough to survive if she had been born. We weren't surprised, 34 weeks would be awfully early for a baby to be mature enough to breathe on her own, but we were relieved that the test came back clear.

On the way home from that appointment my ex husband called. He wanted to discuss some change to our visitation schedule with Jake. He wanted to change the holiday schedule all around, knowing that I was expecting to have this baby by c-section at 39 weeks if everything went well and possibly at any moment if there was an indication that she was in distress. I was furious. I exploded with frustration and burst into tears, which is something I hate doing when I'm dealing with my ex because he never seems to care how I feel. The stress of everything came out in one huge sob. Suddenly it was his fault that I was going through this even though he had nothing to do with it. He told me I was overreacting, and he was right.

Of course I was overreacting. I had just been through an amniocentesis. I never dreamed in a million years that I would need to go through that procedure. My whole life I had been poked and prodded for various issues but never did I expect that. Didn't he realize the mental hell that I was going through? No, of course he didn't and it wasn't his fault. Nobody knew because I didn't tell them. People tried to understand and be supportive but it's nearly impossible unless they have experienced a pregnancy like this themselves. Somehow I took comfort in unloading all of that fear and frustration on him because I knew he would simply hang up the phone and go on with his day. I knew that dumping all of that emotional baggage wouldn't affect him like it would if I spilled it to my family and my close friends. Later that night after I had settled down I called him back. I told him that I was sorry that I had broken down and in a more rational tone explained why it had hit me so hard.

Changing the visitation wasn't something worth getting upset over, and that was his point. He was right, it wasn't but when you like order and schedules like I do that was the straw that broke the camel's back. Everything that we were dealing with in this pregnancy was a curve ball, so even the slightest change to anything else in life was magnified. It's amazing how frustrated you can become when you are dealing with something of such a serious nature and everyone around you is going on with life as usual. There is a fine balance between extreme stress and jealousy that is hard to maintain, and even harder for anyone else not going through it to understand. It is an extremely private journey that can suddenly turn very public if you reach your stress threshold. Looking back I don't know how I managed to avoid yelling at every person I came in contact with, especially when I would have to deal with grown adults who would whine about the most petty things and do it with a smile on my face.

Chapter 9

What Glow?

I had severe post-partum depression with the birth of my son. I had wanted a baby so badly and after he was born I wanted nothing to do with him. I knew that something was seriously wrong when I would sit and fantasize about ways I could hurt myself. This was the strangest feeling because I knew I wasn't myself. I knew I loved my son and I was a good mom. It felt like the real me was buried deep inside and was watching the depressed me living my life, it was very unsettling.

During my pregnancy with Maddie I suffered from depression again. I didn't expect to feel this way before she was born, and was worried that it might be worse after her birth. Getting out of bed during my pregnancy took so much willpower. I had trained myself to take comfort in my moments of self pity and it was a hard habit to break. I privately wondered what second pregnancies felt like when they were normal. Does it feel as exciting as the first? Is it normal to not be as excited for subsequent pregnancies? I had no idea. None of my friends or family members had gone through this. We had nobody that we could turn to for moral support – at least nobody who could carry us through and tell us that there was a light at the end of the tunnel. All we had was each other and I'm thankful that Brandon was there because without him I don't know if I could have gotten out of bed each morning.

What do you do when you're faced with a problem like this? Some women may find comfort in a support group or their women's group at church. I'm more inclined to hold things in, put on the brave face and make light of a situation while I'm quietly breaking down inside. Pride and courage are good traits to have; they were instilled in me at a very early age. They can, however, be detrimental when you reach a bridge that you cannot cross alone. I thank God everyday that he gave me Brandon. His love got me through the hardest days when I cried so hard I ran out of tears. If you've ever been scared like this you know the kind of cry I'm talking about. You tremble so hard your insides shake. You cry so deeply that no sound and no tears escape. You fight to catch your breath and once you do you feel like you've been hit by a train.

Brandon was my lighthouse through the storm. He always knew just what I was thinking, and could read me like a book. He picked up the pieces and stepped in as an instant Dad when it came to Jake. When I just couldn't deal with anything anymore, Brandon stepped in and made sure Jake had everything that he needed. I am so grateful for him and hope that someday I can be a pillar of strength for him in return. He even has an uncanny ability to know when I'm crying on the other end of the phone. It's like he can hear my tear drops falling even though I'm trying to conceal them.

If I hadn't been so lucky to have Brandon, I don't know what I would've done. Our doctors were amazing but I probably couldn't have drawn much more support from them than they provided in our appointments. They are flooded with patients and time is a privilege. I actually feel sympathy for doctors who handle high risk pregnancies. Not every scenario has a happy ending and their ability to offer strength and hope despite the heartbreak they see during their careers amaze me. We were blessed to have such patient doctors.

We were almost in the home stretch. Our friends Val and Leyla threw us a baby shower and my Mom and sister came up from Arizona, I was completely surprised. My HR department also threw us a baby shower. I was pregnant with the fourth HR baby that year. There would be a total of eight HR babies by the time the baby wave had passed. In my office alone three of us were pregnant. Our babies were born within five months of each other. Having other pregnant women around helped a lot, especially the first time moms. Everything was new to them and they asked questions. Through all of the unknowns we had been facing, answering their questions made me feel like I had a brain again. I loved sharing tips and ideas with them, telling them which products I thought were useless and which ones I couldn't live without was so much fun. I felt useful again, something I hadn't felt in months. It energized me and helped me get excited about having another baby, and not a moment too soon!

I became more fascinated with Maddie's development as the weeks passed and she grew closer to full term. I wanted to know how well she would do if she was born prematurely. Each week I would research the statistics for survival if a baby was born then. Her chances improved by the day; and that was a welcome change from the way things had been going.

Our doctor's visits really turned into information gathering sessions. We would go with questions prepared and build up courage in the waiting room to ask them. We would try to be quick with our inquiries because we didn't want to be a nuisance, but needed some form of peace of mind. After each appointment with the perinatologist we would get in our cars and drive home. On the drive home I would always call my parents and would fill them in on the details of the appointment, I held nothing back. We are an honest family and we don't keep things from each other.

My Mom has deep faith and when I would get angry that we were going through so many complications, she would remind me that God would never give us more than we could handle. She was right. Her prayers got us through the most difficult days. My Dad is one of my best friends. I can talk to him about anything and he is always honest with me even when it's hard to hear. His support gave me the courage that I so desperately needed.

The news of the complications was as hard on our families as it was on us. They bought things for the baby but didn't want to give them to us until we knew she was going to make it. In hindsight, that was bittersweet. The gesture was extremely thoughtful because we wouldn't have to look at baby things if the unthinkable happened. On the other hand, being forced to prepare for her arrival may have been enough to snap me out of my depression, especially since I couldn't muster up the motivation to do it myself.

We finally started working on the nursery. Jake, Brandon and I painted and placed wallpaper dragonflies on the wall. We put Maddie's crib together and assembled each piece of her baby gear. Jake helped as much as he could, at least as long as his attention span would allow. I was beginning to feel comfortable preparing for Maddie, I even went through the baby clothes that we had received and got them washed and put away in her room. Her nursery was more than just a room now, it looked warm and welcoming and I felt happy there.

My sister made little wooden dragonflies and painted them purple and yellow. She wrote Maddie's name on them and we hung them up on her window. Now it really looked like a little girl's bedroom. Her white crib looked so perfect against the pale yellow walls and the dragonflies appeared to be dancing in anticipation of her arrival. Her nursery became my favorite room in the house.

Chapter 10

Full Term but not Ready

At 37 weeks I decided that I was going to stop working and start my maternity leave. I struggled with this decision ever since I was put on bed rest with pre-term labor. While I felt fine physically, mentally and emotionally it seemed like this pregnancy had lasted forever. I had wanted to work up until Maddie's delivery but at that point we had no idea when that might be. I had been to more than 40 doctor's visits in the last 20 weeks and had reached my breaking point. My last day at work was Friday, December 26th. Yes, I even worked the day after Christmas. I'm crazy, I know.

Taking leave early was a hard thing to do. With Jake, I worked the day that I went into labor. Like I've said before, I like having control over timing and plans. This pregnancy proved to me that so many things are beyond my control. I learned that I needed to surrender and let everything work out the way it was meant to. That Saturday I decided that I was going to enjoy taking my maternity leave early and try to make the best of the remainder of my pregnancy. I wasn't going to get much time to do that!

Monday I had two appointments scheduled. We had one in the morning with our perinatologist and one at 3:00 pm with the OBGYN. Sunday night as I lay in bed Maddie shifted, and it felt like she was doing somersaults. I had never felt anything like that before and it was really disturbing. It wasn't your normal kick or punch. It didn't even feel like she was rolling over, it felt like she was tangled up and trying to release herself. Once she stopped moving the contractions began. I woke Brandon up and told him I was going to lie on the couch and drink some juice to see if they would stop. I took one of the pills to stop the contractions and after a few hours they slowed enough for me to relax and go back to sleep.

Monday morning I called the OBGYN's office to speak with the nurse and tell her what had happened. She said I shouldn't have taken the medication this late in the pregnancy. I was angry. What was I supposed to do?

We knew that Maddie's lungs weren't mature enough to be born and that they didn't want her delivered now. If they were going to give me steroids to mature her lungs they would have to stop labor from progressing anyway. I couldn't win.

The nurse told me to go to my normal appointments and have the perinatologist monitor my contractions, and not to eat or drink anything incase they decided to deliver today. At that point it was 9:00 am. I had been having contractions 5 minutes apart for 11 hours. I should've gone straight to the hospital but we had already been there twice with pre-term labor and I didn't want to go through that nightmare again unless it was time. I hadn't eaten or had anything to drink since 11:30 Sunday night.

By noon we were at the perinatologist's office. We were called back to be monitored and when I saw our regular nurse I burst into tears. Seeing a friendly face was so comforting. She asked how I was and reassured me that everything would be ok as she hooked me up to the monitor and left the room. The contractions were measuring off the chart. The nurse checked my cervix and fortunately I wasn't dilated. She said she would call my doctor and tell him what my readings were. By 3:00 pm we were at our next appointment with the OBGYN. 17 hours of steady contractions had gone by with no relief in sight. I wasn't supposed to go into labor; I was supposed to have a "scheduled" c-section. This was ridiculous. We waited to see the doctor and then it was our turn.

The nurse asked if the perinatologist's office did an amnio to see if the baby's lungs were mature, I told her they hadn't. She told me that I was going to have to go back and have them do one. I was so upset that I told her if I had this baby in the car driving all over town I was going to be pissed. She quickly went to get the doctor.

The doctor came in and told me what the results of the monitoring had said. His opinion was that I was just having nuisance contractions. Once again I lost it. I know he is the doctor, and that this is what he does every day. He's delivered hundreds of babies but none of them have come out of his body. I knew what I was talking about. I told him how long the contractions had been going on and asked him why I was being allowed to labor when I was supposed to have a c-section. I needed to know what our plan was. After some short discussion he left to call the hospital and schedule the c-section. He came back and told us we were scheduled at 5:00 that night. I had no idea if they would do another amnio to check her lung maturity or what would happen, but we were off and running.

Chapter 11

The End of a Long Journey

We drove across the street to a shopping center and grabbed some last minute items. We called our families and told them the news. I had made a huge mistake that weekend. Brandon's Mom had booked airfare to be in town that day and we told her to change the date because we didn't know when the delivery would be. Now it was happening and I felt horrible. Once again instead of letting things happen I had tried to intervene and things went awry. My parents got bags packed and started the drive up to Las Vegas. Brandon's Mom booked new airfare and his Dad and Stepmom booked train tickets. Jake was with his dad and older sisters and would get to come up to the hospital after the delivery. It was reassuring to know that he would be preoccupied and taken care of while we were making sure the baby got here safely.

Fortunately we had packed our bags and had them in the car so we didn't have to run back home to get anything. We left the store and went back to the hospital. Up in labor and delivery we got checked in and made ourselves comfortable in the labor room. Our doctor wanted to monitor me one more time to see if my contractions continued before we went into surgery. My contractions remained off the charts, and I went through three bags of IV fluid. After all the concern about another amnio they never performed one while we were at the hospital.

At 4:45 pm my doctor made the decision that we would go ahead with the c-section. The nurse removed the monitors and brought in paperwork for me to sign. She gave Brandon scrubs to wear in the operating room and he went to change in the bathroom. I could tell he was nervous about the surgery, especially when he popped his head out of the bathroom to tell me that he had forgotten to put on underwear. I had to laugh.

To maintain his modesty he decided to put the scrub pants on over his jeans. Again, I had to laugh. Only Brandon!

I wasn't as nervous about the surgery because I knew what to expect from Jake's birth. There was one difference though. This time they would be doing a spinal block instead of an epidural like I had with Jake and I am highly sensitive if not allergic to morphine. They walked me into the operating room and had me sit on the table. The anesthesiologist had assured me that a spinal block only had a small dose of morphine and it shouldn't cause any problems. Brandon later told me that he watched the anesthesiologist attempt to find a "pocket" in my spine five times before finally getting the block in place. I should have trusted my instinct and told him I wanted an epidural instead. The morphine made me vomit immediately. Thankfully I hadn't had anything to eat or drink in nearly 24 hours so it was more of a dry heave. I told the anesthesiologist that I wasn't feeling well and right as I was about to pass out he put something in my IV that made me better. The whole time Brandon was watching from the door waiting to come in, he looked so concerned.

Brandon came in and sat next to me and gave me a kiss as they started to deliver Maddie. He stood up just as his first born made her entry into the world and followed her to have her vitals checked. He brought her over to me and I gave her a kiss, then he and the nurses left with my baby girl, they were headed to the NICU. Maddie's lungs were not mature, so she had lots of fluid in them. She was struggling to breathe and I was lying on the operating table clueless. The doctors and nurses tried to keep the mood light and talked to me about parenthood and the beauty of a new baby. I had no idea how she was, or even that there were problems.

My doctors closed my incision and they prepared me to be taken to recovery. I still hadn't held my daughter and nearly two hours later, Brandon walked into the room with bloodshot eyes. The look on his face scared me to death; I thought our daughter had died. He explained to me that she was struggling to breathe and that she was covered with tubes. I was devastated. We had made it this far, we couldn't lose her now. I wanted to see my baby but I wasn't allowed to get out of bed yet and she couldn't leave the NICU. I didn't get to hold my daughter until 24 hours after her birth. The first moments that a mother and baby have after birth were postponed.

The nurses moved me to the final recovery room where I would stay until I was discharged. It was huge, there was enough room for another hospital bed but instead there was a couch and several chairs. That became Brandon's sanctuary. Between his visits to see the baby he would come back and rest on the couch next to me. I wanted to see my little girl so badly, but I had to settle for digital pictures that he took while he was in the NICU with her. I'm thankful that the nurses let him take those pictures, as they are very protective of the babies and any flash would disturb them.

I couldn't believe that we had made it, and that Maddie didn't have any problems related to my infection with fifth disease. We were literally in the home stretch and her last obstacle was learning how to breathe on her own. I knew we had a tough little girl on our hands, but biology can be quite an opponent. I thought about parents who have extremely premature babies and realized that the chances of survival are improving for even the tiniest newborns; so at three weeks premature she should have pretty good odds.

Our little girl was going to make it, I was certain. Brandon would go to see her and give me updates on her condition. I decided to try to pump breast milk for her but due to my breast reduction the year earlier I wasn't successful. I was prepared for that and we had already decided that formula feeding was ok with us.

Chapter 12

Meeting My Daughter

Later when I was allowed to get out of bed, we made the slow journey down the hall to the NICU. As Brandon pushed my wheelchair into the nursery I could hear faint cries. I grew anxious because I wasn't sure what to expect when I got to see my baby girl. The babies were so tiny they sounded like kittens crying. We washed our hands and made our way to Madelyn's isolette. 5 pounds, 9 ounces and 18 inches long. She was a pound lighter than her brother was when he was born. Unbelievably I was able to look past all of the tubes and wires and saw only my beautiful daughter. Finally the bonding had begun. I had a daughter!

As I looked at her full head of brown hair and perfect little features I realized what it meant to be the mother of a little girl. She was delicate, fragile and at the same time tough as nails. I held her in my arms and looked at her sweet little face, she was so precious. She had the most amazing scent too, that new baby smell is the best. The nurses told us that she was really loud when she would suck on her pacifier, she made a clicking sound. We had to laugh because you wouldn't expect that from such a small baby. I had given birth to a survivor. She was just a day old and she was already my hero. In that moment I made a silent promise to Maddie. I promised that even though I couldn't protect her from fifth disease when I was pregnant I would spend the rest of my life protecting her – but first she needed to get better so we could go home.

She made the strangest gasping noise sometimes, it almost sounded like someone had surprised her and she was startled. We weren't sure if this was because of her difficulty breathing, or if it was just some cute little quirk she had. Every time she would make that noise we would stop what we were doing and double check that she was ok, just to be on the safe side.

The nurses in the NICU were so good to us. They were patient and understanding when we had questions. Well, all of them but one. One nurse had a very "different" personality. She would tune in to every word Brandon and I said to each other regarding our baby girl and would interrupt and correct us. For instance, Maddie glanced up at Brandon and it looked like she was looking right at him. Brandon and I are both intelligent people and we know that newborns don't have the ability to focus their eyesight, and they really can't see much for some time. I happened to say, "Look, she's looking at you!" What a mistake. That nurse jumped all over me that newborn babies can't see anything and they don't know what they are looking at. What a wonderful way to ruin such a sweet moment. She almost acted as if we were coming to see her child and were creating an inconvenience for her. She was pretty irritating, but after the first few remarks she made, we regrouped and took great joy in irritating her right back.

That afternoon Brandon picked Jake up from school and brought him to the hospital. Jake was very cautious of the hospital since he had spent nearly a week in one several months earlier for MRSA. He entered the room and was very concerned about where the baby was so we got up and walked down the hall with him towards the NICU. Jake couldn't go in the nursery or hold his baby sister and that broke my heart, but Maddie's isolette was up against the glass and the family got a great view of her. Brandon and I were in the nursery with Maddie and we held her up so that Jake could get a better look while my Dad held him so he could peer into the window. He looked so scared and concerned because she still had wires and tubes attached to her. He wanted to hold her more than anything but that was going to have to wait until we got to take her home.

That night there was an influx of pregnant women trying to have New Year's babies. Our normal, amazing night shift nurse had been called away to help in Labor and Delivery. Before she left she made one more round and gave me a dose of pain medication. That was around 5:30 pm. That was the last we saw of her until the next evening. In her absence, another nurse was pulled from a different department and assigned to postpartum recovery. She never came in to check on me or to give me my scheduled pain medication. At 5:00 am I tried to get out of bed to use the restroom and nearly passed out from the pain. It was unbearable. I will never forget the feeling of my muscles ripping and burning like that. Brandon helped me to the bathroom and then went out in the hall to raise hell.

The substitute nurse came back in and chastised me for not taking my scheduled medication. I was in so much pain that I snapped at her and told her it was her job to keep up the medication schedule, not mine. We told the charge nurse on the day shift and she passed it on to the charge nurse on the night shift. Our regular night shift nurse came back and apologized profusely. I am so glad that Brandon was there to help; he slept on the little sofa that was in the recovery room so that he wouldn't have to leave us. I still don't know how he folded himself up and fit on that thing, but he managed to.

Maddie's vitals began to improve, but she was having trouble eating. Her pediatrician suggested a sensitive formula and she improved even more. That was day number two. She was doing better by the hour, and eventually was able to have the monitors removed when we held her. The little blood pressure cuff was so tiny it looked like a toy. We spent New Year's Eve in the hospital and my parents brought us sparkling cider and plastic cups so that we could still celebrate. Our nurse brought in a gift that she had made for all of the parents. It was a plastic cup with chocolate in it and a sash that said Baby's First New Year 2009. It was so cute that we saved it for Maddie. January 1, 2009 my doctor talked about releasing me, and I was ready to go home but I had one requirement; my daughter was going with me. My biggest fear was that she would have to stay in the NICU and we would go home with empty arms. I couldn't bear the thought of that. My doctor was kind enough to make sure that the neonatologist and pediatrician cleared Maddie for release before he approved my discharge. That night we learned that we would all be going home, that was the best news we had heard since we found out we were having a baby!!

Chapter 13

Meeting her new Family

Brandon and I were in the NICU when we found out that we were being sent home and my parents were waiting for us in our hospital room. The next thing they saw was me pushing her isolette down the hallway and into my hospital room. This was the first time she was able to leave the confines of the NICU. We told my parents that she was being discharged too and you could feel the electricity in the room. We were finally experiencing the normal joys of a new baby. Brandon and my Dad went downstairs to make sure the car seat base was properly installed and my mom and I packed up our belongings to prepare for the drive home. Dad and Brandon came back upstairs and told us about the angel at our car. As Brandon opened the back hatch of the SUV he looked down to see a window cling of a child praying staring up at him, he picked it up and tucked it away as a keepsake. We got Maddie dressed in her going home outfit and it swallowed her, she was so tiny. We had brought a few preemie outfits but we were so flustered by the whole situation that we couldn't get it on her. Everything felt like it was happening so fast.

We placed her in the car seat and she looked like a little porcelain doll. She still had some jaundice and would have to be seen by the doctor the next day. One last quick glance around the room and then we all walked to the elevator and made our way through the lobby. It felt so good to be going home, and at the same time I was afraid we weren't ready. We drove home and my parents followed us. We brought Maddie into the house and showed her around. Mom and Dad got to hold her and enjoy her without the boundaries of the NICU. The next day we took her to the pediatrician to be evaluated for her jaundice. She needed to have some blood work done to make sure that she was getting better. Brandon took her and tried to locate a lab that was open and had her blood sample taken. We gave Maddie short sun baths and she loved it. We were fortunate that she didn't need any other medical intervention for the jaundice, the sun bathing helped and it cleared up on its own.

Jake stayed with his Dad until the next weekend and when he came home he was excited to have a baby sister. He was so gentle and helped us with everything she needed. He wanted to watch every diaper change, and loved taking them to the trash as long as they only had pee in them. He watched us give her a bath and kissed her forehead as often as he could. It was heartwarming to watch him with her. He even wanted us to put a sleeping bag down in our room so that he could sleep in there with us. I explained that the baby was going to be sleeping there in the bassinet and she might cry a lot at night. He didn't care. Amazingly, he slept all through the night even though we were up every two to three hours with her for feedings.

He had no sibling rivalry; he was calm, gentle and protective of her already. I couldn't have been more proud of my son. Jake wasn't too sure about holding her though, to this day it's still a work in progress. We have several pictures of him holding her with a scared look on his face and after about two seconds he would say, "Ok, get her off!" Although he is timid about holding her, Maddie loves being around her brother. She loves hearing his voice and calms down whenever he is around. She was the perfect baby right off the bat and we knew just how lucky we were.

Brandon's Dad and stepmom Katy came to visit from Missouri next. They traveled by train to see their new granddaughter and we were so glad that they did. It was really nice to see them and so much fun to watch them interact with both of the kids. They took turns trying to steal Maddie from each other and Brandon and I just sat back and watched. Later all of them gathered in the kitchen and gave Maddie a bath. I still remember watching Brandon and his Dad huddled together to bathe her. They were talking to each other and I couldn't quite hear what they were saying but I was overcome with emotion just watching it. Brandon loves his Dad so much, and it's evident how much he misses him. They share so many mannerisms that sometimes I have to laugh and tell him, "I just saw your Dad!" when he's playing with Jake. I know that our kids are going to love Brandon the same way that he loves his Dad. His love is real, and pure, not forced or obligatory.

After Brandon's Dad and Katy went home, his Mom came out from Missouri to see Maddie. Jake was back with his Dad for her visit, so he missed out on seeing her. This was her first granddaughter. She had told me that when she was pregnant with Brandon she had wished he was a little girl. Watching her with Maddie was so sweet. They look so much alike, dark hair and deep blue eyes. She watched the baby for us and Brandon and I went to lunch all by ourselves. It was really strange, but really nice too. We had a great time while his Mom was with us; we ate, drank and watched our favorite news show together. We started planning our trip out to Missouri with the kids because we realized how much the family would miss seeing the baby.

Shortly after Brandon's Mom left, we went down to Arizona to see the rest of my family and let my sister see her niece. Her sons just loved having the baby around and wanted a little sister of their own. My Grandpa got to hold his fifth great-granddaughter. We have great pictures from that trip.

We met with my best friend Elizabeth and she got to meet her namesake for the first time. Her little girl Sophie got to see Maddie too and was extremely jealous when Elizabeth held her. She kept saying, "Mommy, No!" It was so cute!

Next we went back to Missouri. I have never flown with kids before, so this was a new experience. Jake was so excited about the trip, he couldn't wait to go on an airplane. I was incredibly stressed out by the thought of flying with them. I put off packing until the night before, and that was a huge mistake. I was so stressed that I didn't even want to go. The next morning we woke up and finished getting ready. We made our way to the airport with what seemed like a ton of stuff crammed into one big red suitcase. Thankfully it weighed less than 50 lbs; otherwise we would have been in big trouble. Jake had a little backpack with his snacks and we had Maddie's diaper bag.

We arrived in Springfield and Brandon's brother and nephew met us at the airport. Then his mom arrived and we headed back to her house. That week was a whirlwind. I got to meet some of Brandon's friends that he's had for ages, and his best friend Chad got to hold the daughter Brandon never thought he would have. Brandon's stepdad Jimmy took right to Maddie and rocked her in his chair for hours after we all went to bed. Watching him with her was so sweet! We took the kids over to Brandon's Grandma's house and she held her with the biggest smile on her face. I took so many pictures that day. Brandon's cousins came over with their kids and the kids played outside while the rest of us were in the house with the baby. Everyone accepted Jake and me right away and for that I will always be thankful. We immediately felt like a part of the family, and that's rare when you have a blended family like we do. I hope to raise my children to be as accepting as they were towards us, because at the end of the day family is all that really matters.

We wrapped up the trip and headed back home to start our normal everyday life. It felt so nice to be home, and to have our kids. Our family was complete. Maddie continued to grow and thrive. She is five months old now and Jake is getting ready to celebrate his 5th birthday.

Chapter 14

Our Happy Ending

I look back and I can't believe the road we traveled during our pregnancy with Maddie. The expense of the doctors' visits alone was unreal. Although the cost was high, it was worth every penny to have our little girl safe and sound at home. We look forward to watching her develop and grow, along with Jake's help of course! Maddie loves to put her hands in Jake's hair. She gets the biggest smile on her face. Jake kisses her hands and feet and loves to show her his dinosaur toys. She watches him with wide eyes trying to see everything he does.

Maddie is the textbook Daddy's Girl, she can't get enough of Brandon and it appears that he feels the same way about her. I watch as he feeds her a bottle and her tiny little hands move slowly back and forth on top of his. She wraps her little fingers around one of his and snuggles in beside him. Brandon has an amazing ability to make her smile, and her giggles are infectious when he makes her laugh. When he carries her through the house all I can see is her tiny little face peering over his shoulder. She wears a look of total contentment on her face, and occasionally when I catch her eye she gives me a coy little smile as if she's taunting me because she has all of his attention.

That little girl, although only a few months old; has the ability to mesmerize each of us. She has become very vocal and loves to see how high her voice will go. Just the other day she called my Mom "ding ding". I laughed so hard I almost cried. Diaper changes are becoming more and more challenging now that she is eating baby food, which we decided to make ourselves for cost effectiveness as well as nutritional value. She has also started to roll away in the middle of diaper changes, which is so much fun!

Her hair has grown long enough that I can put a bow in it, and I just love doing that! We want to have her ears pierced but I keep talking myself out of taking her, just the thought of it breaks my heart even though I know it won't hurt her. She's become my little buddy, we talk about how wonderful her Daddy is and how someday I hope she finds a man as kind and loving as he is. She always smiles during those conversations; I know she can understand me.

She has begun to use a saucer now and Jake just loves spending time with her when she's sitting in it. He plays with the toys on the saucer with her and explains what every piece is. She looks at him with wide eyes, as if she's soaking in every word that comes out of his mouth. Jake gives her the sweetest kisses on the forehead and is incredibly gentle with her considering his age. The other day the kids were in the living room and Barney was on TV. I was in the kitchen and I overheard Maddie starting to cry. Jake chimed in and said in his sweetest big brother voice, "don't worry Madwin, he's not real". I smiled and felt so proud of my little man. He was already coming to her rescue. She settled right down and continued to play with the toys on her saucer.

She can sit with just a bit of support, and loves to grab my lips and nose when I'm feeding her. She gets the funniest look on her face like she knows exactly what she's doing but at the same time she's so innocent that I couldn't possibly get upset.

Right now we're enduring the long road to cutting the first tooth. I feel so bad for her, she is always chewing on her fingers and without a bib her outfits would always be dripping wet. As much as I look forward to her passing that milestone to relieve some of her discomfort, it will be a bittersweet moment as she begins to emerge from infancy. Soon will come the days of frantically trying to keep her out of the kitchen and away from all things unsafe. Not long after that we will watch her try to take her first steps.

I look back and I wish I could rewind the last year. Knowing what I know now I would handle my high risk pregnancy differently. I wouldn't take for granted the kicks and the punches while she was in the womb. I would have continued to plan and enjoy my pregnancy, living only in that moment without being distracted with the "what ifs". I would let my faith rest in God and trust that my physicians would be able to get us through the pregnancy with minimal complications. Hindsight is always 20/20 and we handled our pregnancy with Maddie as best as we knew how at that point in time.

So that's our story. In just over a year we went from excitement over an impending pregnancy, to heartache and depression over complications, and finally to the joy and elation of having a healthy baby girl. I am grateful that we had the support of family, friends and two wonderful doctors and their staff along the way. We couldn't have done it without them. It was a long journey and although there were many bumps in the road it made us a stronger family. Brandon and I will be married in a few weeks and we have a birthday party to plan for Jake.

Next thing you know it will be time to celebrate Maddie's first birthday. I'm already planning her first birthday cake. It's so much fun having a little girl!! It took me a while, but I've finally been able to let go of the fear that we might lose her. We're the normal American family with two children. We have good days, and we have bad days but no matter what happens all that matters is that we have each other.

Chapter 15

Advice from Someone who's Been There

So many nights I tossed and turned wishing that there was someone I could turn to who had magic advice. I mentioned earlier in the book that none of our friends or family had been through a pregnancy like this one; so we were left to our own devices in order to get by. This chapter is written specifically for those who are going through a high risk or complicated pregnancy; in the hopes that you will not feel as left out and alone as I did. Nothing here is intended to be construed as medical advice; I aim only to offer comfort and support to those in need.

If you are diagnosed with a condition during pregnancy; or if you discover that there is a complication with your pregnancy do your best to keep a level head. This may sound easier said than done, but if you are able to think clearly you will fare much better than if you allow the situation to get the best of you. Find a healthy balance between living day to day and continuing to prepare for the birth of your beautiful baby. You're working hard to help your little one grow, it's a thankless job but it's the best one you'll ever have!

Try as hard as you can to let people help you. I had to learn the hard way that my stubborn pride was only hurting me in the long run. Your friends and family will only be able to understand how you are feeling and dealing with your pregnancy if you are honest with them. Sometimes there aren't family members or close friends nearby, I understand that because that's the situation that Brandon and I faced. I should have looked for other mothers in my area who were experiencing similar issues with their pregnancy.

I may have been able to connect with other women who felt the same way that I did. One would think that pregnancy is the one thing that can bring women together; but call a pregnancy complicated and suddenly you will feel completely alienated and only able to relate to your doctors.

Having physicians you trust is key! Whether you are using a Midwife, an OBGYN or if you are seeing a specialist like I was; make sure that you are able to communicate well with them. Facing challenges with a pregnancy is stressful, and sometimes the lingo, tests and diagnoses can be very confusing. If your health care provider doesn't communicate with you clearly it will make things that much more difficult. Of course it goes both ways; you should feel comfortable enough asking questions, making comments about how you feel etc; if you don't then it's time to find another health care provider. There is nothing wrong with changing doctors like I did. I wasn't confident with my first OBGYN's capabilities and she left much to be desired with her bedside manner. Finding a new doctor put my mind at ease, especially when we found out we needed special care.

Looking back I wish I had kept a pregnancy journal. Sure, it wouldn't be something that I would necessarily want my daughter to read someday; but it would have helped me release some of the fear and anger over the situation. I would have been able to go back and re-read my journal entries and digest my emotions. I think that having a journal would have helped Brandon too because I know he was trying his best to hide any fear or anger that he was feeling. He did a great job too because he never let it show. Self restraint isn't always healthy when it comes to dealing with these sorts of things. Sometimes you need to be able to have a release of sorts. A journal would have been the perfect thing for us.

We obviously did lots of research about my infection from fifth disease and the affect it could have on the baby. This is something that you may or may not feel comfortable with. Some would rather let the health care professionals worry about what could or could not happen and just make their appointments as required. Others may find some comfort in learning all of the ins and outs of the complications. To each their own on this one; if you feel comfortable looking up a few things then I think it's a great idea. The moment you begin to feel depressed or more concerned than expected I think you should stop researching and focus on your health and the health of your baby. Knowledge can be power, but use it wisely.

Speaking of depression, if you start to feel hopeless and can't find the motivation to get out of bed each day you should really find someone to talk to. If you don't feel comfortable seeking the help of a counselor you may feel comfortable speaking with someone from a church group if you belong to one, or seeking support in online communities. Many cities have Mom's groups where you can meet with other women in person. If you don't feel comfortable with that you can also find people to talk to in Mom related forums online.

I unfortunately did not practice what I preach, and I wish I had because our pregnancy with Maddie was so mentally and emotionally exhausting for both of us; having someone to vent to who was removed from the situation would have been so helpful. It's always easier for someone to help you through things if they have been through it before, and seeing the situation from their perspective.

Never be ashamed of how you feel, and never feel guilty for wishing you could go back and change things so that you wouldn't have been classified as high risk. Some things are beyond our control and that was a hard fact for me to accept. I had Supermom syndrome and thought that I had to handle it all myself; all the while with a brave face on. This is something that I still struggle with and it will slowly make you miserable. We are all human! You are perfectly normal if you have a meltdown now and then! Heck, after what you are going through you deserve a good cry!

Being a mother is one of life's toughest jobs. It is severely underpaid and many times underappreciated. Don't feel like you are a horrible mother if you don't feel ready to deal with your pregnancy or if you are having a hard time preparing for you child while dealing with complications. Having a baby can be frightening. Your life is changing and in turn creating yet another life. Anyone who tells you they weren't the slightest bit nervous or afraid when they found out they were having a baby is not telling you the whole truth. We all get scared, for various reasons; and you are entitled to get scared too. You will be amazed by how much you can handle, the fear doesn't last long.

Motherhood is a rite of passage, and I've learned that even after having one child, subsequent pregnancies can be a different test of your fortitude. Each pregnancy is different and challenging in its own way and all of them deserve to be cherished no matter the situation. Try as best you can to find positive things about your pregnancy. It may be hard to do at first but focusing on the good rather than the bad will become a healthy habit! If you have other children try to focus on preparing them for a sibling. We were fortunate that our son was young enough to be extremely intrigued by the thought of a new baby. If you have older children you might have a tougher time getting them involved with preparation; but it doesn't hurt to try.

You can ask them how they feel about having a younger sibling; or another younger sibling if that is the case. Allow them to be honest with you without getting upset with them. Maybe they are dealing with the same fears that you are. If they are old enough to understand that you have a high risk pregnancy I'm sure they have their own fears and concerns. It may help you if you are able to share your feelings with your children too. Always keep in mind that children are just that; children. Being honest with your children is a wonderful thing, but take care not to unload too much on them. Regardless of their age they want you to be happy and often times are struggling with their own feelings about the situation themselves. They may wind up feeling like they have to make things better for you. Remember, no matter how difficult it is to handle your fear or your stress; you are the parent.

If you find that you are getting upset easily and it's affecting your children or others in your household; make a plan to talk to them when you aren't feeling as upset. With a clear head sit down with them and explain in an age appropriate manner just how you're feeling and why you react to things the way that you do. I'm sure that they will appreciate your honesty and it will help them understand what's going on the next time that you get upset about something. Then the ball is in your court. Try to find a way to catch yourself before you get upset and think about what has made you react that way. Anger and frustration can happen very quickly and it may take a while to get the hang of censoring yourself like this. If nothing else, after you've cooled down jot down what you got upset about. You can always go back and read it later. You may be surprised how insignificant issues seem once you've calmed down.

Never underestimate your ability to cope. We are women and we are strong! We have the ability to give life to another human being, and there is nothing more beautiful than that.

Chapter 16

Coping with Loss

Brandon and I were fortunate that Maddie survived my pregnancy and is a healthy little girl today. We know that many parents are not as lucky. The first miscarriage that I had years earlier devastated me. My ex husband didn't know how to console me, and I was heartbroken. I was only about six weeks pregnant, and had not seen a doctor yet. I had been excited about the pregnancy even though I had wanted to wait until Jake was older before adding to my family.

We went to dinner one night and I went to the restroom because I was having some cramps. I was losing the baby. I told my ex and he went home with Jake. I drove myself to the emergency room; and there I sat, alone and dying on the inside. I hadn't even seen an ultrasound of the baby yet, but I was already attached.

I grieved for that baby for two years and then it happened again; this time with Brandon. Losing a child is devastating, no matter when it occurs. When you lose a baby during pregnancy you feel cheated because you never got a chance to see who your child would become. Their personality will forever be a mystery.

There is nothing wrong with mourning the loss of your child, but be careful and watch for signs that your grief has turned to depression; there is a very fine line between the two. If you begin to feel like you aren't handling your grief well, make sure you speak with someone; your health care provider is an excellent person to start with.

If you feel the need, give your child a name. This is something that can help some women. I personally couldn't do that. I was very early in pregnancy and we hadn't discussed names. I hadn't had an ultrasound, so making a connection and a bond with both the babies hadn't really happened yet. Like I said before, each of us is different. Some women may want to name a baby no matter when a miscarriage occurs. My point is; do whatever helps you get through.

Always, always remember that everything happens for a reason; no matter how difficult and painful it is. Had I not had two miscarriages I may not have my beautiful Madelyn today. Faith will always bring you peace. If you believe that you will never have to face more than you can handle, you will be ok! Have the courage to stand up to the obstacles in your way and you will overcome them. Always keep your heart and mind open and you will be blessed with a beautiful baby, by whatever means you decide is best for you.

Thank you for allowing us to share our experiences with you. I hope that our story will help you or someone you love get through your own personal journey.

www.ingramcontent.com/pod-product-compliance
Lightning Source LLC
LaVergne TN
LVHW011407080426
835511LV00005B/418